Essential Learning Wisdom For
Back-to-College & Career Adults

THE
KANGAROO
METHOD

How To Unlock Your Verbal Intelligence
& Become The Person You Most Want To Be

W9-CNC-005

by

DONALD RUSSELL WOODRUFF

The Professional Vocabulary Institute

Contents

To JoAnn

Introduction

ONE day I was surprised to discover there is *another* Kangaroo Method that serves to make people's lives better. That method is a way to nurture and breastfeed a baby by placing a newborn, skin-to-skin, on its mother's chest, just as kangaroo moms do. My Kangaroo Method is a way to read and learn better by becoming genuinely word smart and thereby jumping several levels toward what you really wish to achieve in life.

Most back-to-college adults are able to sail through boundless chapters by their favorite authors although they admit they are far less competent when reading more substantial information. In fact, I have met a surprising number of remarkably intelligent people who hate to read. When discussing work-related reports and other required reading, they use words and phrases such as "dry," "boring," "overly wordy," and "time consuming" to express their feelings toward such material. Others find it difficult to maintain their concentration for any length of time no matter what they read.

Many otherwise successful adults confess they never quite finish what they start. Their bookcases become filled with partially read books about business, personal growth, money and investing, science and technology, and religion and spirituality. Although willing to learn, they often don't get beyond the first few chapters. They may tune out several times while reading down a page and forget what they read. Some may also wonder if they have undiagnosed adult ADD or ADHD.

With today's extensive online information, we have instant access to far more facts and ideas than even Albert Einstein might have dreamt of. For those who have honed their research skills, the ability to hunt down information on the Internet is fast and focused. But statistics suggest that there may be as few as five percent of American adults who can efficiently skim a 300-page text to capture the answers they need to pass an exam or move forward on a project.

According to U.S. reading proficiency tests conducted over the last 20 years, the scores of 95% of young adults have been less than top notch, with almost 70% scoring below the national proficiency level. As a whole, adults have been consistently ill equipped to capture and retain key points from books and texts. In today's competitive world, where knowledge in almost every field doubles every year, this can be an extreme disadvantage.

To stay competitive, Americans need to be highly proficient readers. Some who are actively seeking to upgrade their reading skills register for my strategic learning course offered at their local college. They come expecting to learn tricks and fancy techniques enabling them to focus better, read faster, and remember more. But underneath this surface anticipation, most suspect that their reading and vocabulary skills may not be solid enough to succeed. They come to my classes for memory tricks and speed-learning techniques while secretly suspecting that they may have missed the boat on the more fundamental skills that matter most. They are reaching out for solutions.

Past programs on speed-reading, vocabulary enhancement, and accelerated learning have helped but none of these methods focused on the real issue. No one program provided a single, dedicated technique to raise the verbal intelligence of back-to-college and career-minded adults. The vast majority of participants in these programs learned how to read faster but with less comprehension. They learned how to obtain a more impressive-sounding vocabulary but merely by rote. And they learned how to rely on their strongest learning style without being encouraged to also strengthen their weakest. Similar to Western medicine methods that aim at eliminating symptoms rather than addressing root causes, these programs failed by concentrating on superficial fixes.

My Kangaroo Method, in contrast, serves to raise an individual's ability to become genuinely more intelligent. It proves effective in strengthening overall reading fluency, concentration, comprehension, retention, and the ability to apply information to better one's circumstances.

America's problem is not illiteracy. It is that these times require Americans to become highly proficient readers. The solution is to significantly raise verbal intelligence. High verbal intelligence enables a person to cut through information quickly, comprehend in "high definition," retain specific points needed for one's purpose, and put newly acquired knowledge to work.

Although the title might sound like a program designed for school-age kids and teens, I confess I have never had much interest in teaching young people. I become interested when students—of any age—become serious about careers and activities that make a positive difference in their lives and the lives of others. This is the time when individuals recognize a need to upgrade their academic skills. Instead of merely parroting back facts, they start to question and seek answers as their experience and vision mature. And to truly succeed, they become willing to overcome an unseen learning disability that inadvertently took hold as a result of their American education. It is this in-grown disability that causes most people to think they cannot become expert readers.

Hidden Barrier

There exists a hidden barrier to learning, thwarting any sincere attempt to increase one's verbal intelligence. This book explains how to remove this unseen obstacle. There are no required reading exercises, no lengthy vocabulary lists, and no fancy memory techniques.

In addition to the Kangaroo Method, I have included those learning techniques I wish I had known while in school, including a detailed procedure on how to effectively handle information from the written page and how to succeed in college while spending less time reading. It unpacks the art of skill building. And it attempts to communicate a great spiritual insight that may challenge your beliefs about yourself. I decided to include this insight because it is the underlying principle on which the Kangaroo Method is based. But more importantly, I believe this insight will help you pair your self-esteem with advancing degrees of reading proficiency. For this reason, I suggest you approach this book as you would one on *Personal Growth*. Just read along at your leisure and consider how each point relates to your own life.

In this time of scientific and technological advancement, no other skill supersedes the importance of one's ability to fluently grasp and retain pertinent information from the written page. My Kangaroo Method is dedicated to this end.

CHAPTER ONE

Learning Is The Pathway To Becoming The Person You Most Want To Be

JUST like you, I learned to become the person I am today. I have learned that "the mind is not a vessel to be filled, but a fire to be ignited," as the Greek historian, Plutarch [ploo-tahrk] said. Moreover, I have learned how to fire the mind with such clarity that information is able to simultaneously connect throughout my whole brain, giving me profound understandings, enhanced memory, and a heightened aptitude to express my thoughts in words and put what I have learned into action. Past anxiety and uncertainty associated with traditional education is gone. I feel confident and able to understand and retain information from lectures and reading, and the freedom to build new skills. This change in me resulted from the use of a single learning tool that I call the Kangaroo Method.

I have taught this method to thousands of people in

schools and colleges and in corporations and at international learning symposiums. From the results of surveys of more than ten thousand back-to-college and professional adults from around the country, I am convinced that the Kangaroo Method will unlock your verbal intelligence and give you the intellectual boost you have long been seeking. Imagine capturing how-to information, studying for an exam, or reading a challenging book in high definition. The insights and techniques I share here are those I hope you will put into your own words and share with your children.

As Simple as a Cup of Tea

Think of a cup filled with hot tea. Add some honey and stir it in, noticing how the honey dissolves into the tea.

Read a book and observe some new ideas. Consider these ideas, talk about them with friends and use them to enhance your know-how.

Once the honey is stirred into the cup, has it changed the tea into something new? Of course it has changed. It has become hot, sweetened tea.

Once the ideas you read are thought about and put to use, have you changed? Yes, similar to the change within the tea you too have changed. Oliver Wendell Homes was of the opinion that, "when a mind is stretched to a new idea it never returns to its original dimension."

Once you were a child and then became a teenager. At that time, others helped you to become the person you are today. They took control of your mind. They did so by presenting ideas to you, one-after-another, with the intention of creating the person they wished you to become.

Today, you have long-since taken control of what you stir into yourself. You are the chemist of your own future. You decide on what specific knowledge to integrate within your brain and body to become the person you most want to be.

Key Concept

The key to unlocking verbal intelligence lies within the crossover of words into ideas. When words are adequately known and the subject is akin to something within one's experience, a person is able to reconstruct an author's ideas and thus achieve a smooth and delightful transference of knowledge. Just last century, learning experts referred to this as "the flow state" or "being in the learning zone." I prefer to think of it as reading in high definition. No matter what we call it, it is simply the way a healthy brain learns when it has not been dulled, overwhelmed, or confused.

Do you think it is possible that words serve to both inform and confuse? What results when you attempt to learn from inadequately known words? Is it possible that vaguely defined words cause your mind to dull? Provided ideas are tendered in proper sequence, when you fail to comprehend, is it the idea that is too complex, or could it be poorly known words creating the difficulty?

The key to the world of reading is the well-defined word. Like the result of using perfectly gapped sparkplugs to ignite a combustion engine, well-defined words fire crystal-clear ideas. Once achieved, a masterful vocabulary empowers the language areas of the brain to effectively network with various sensory and memory regions resulting in profound, all-at-once understandings.

As a young adult, I found my English vocabulary to be a mishmash of uncertainties where few words were known to the standard of the Kangaroo Method. Though I was familiar with hundreds of terms, my depth of understanding was horribly lacking. Most words I merely assumed I knew, while in reality I could not define even the most familiar terms. In retrospect, I was blind, and I didn't even know it!

Today, I refer to these inadequately known words as verbal blind spots. These blind spots prevented me from achieving high definition learning. I use the phrase "verbal blind spot" to denote a vocabulary term I assume I know but am unable to verbally define within the context of what I'm reading. I am unable to simply say what the word means. Moreover, I attribute a vast array of symptoms (including sleepiness, confusion, poor concentration and memory, and a general lack of applicable understanding) to be more caused by these so-called verbal blind spots than any other single source.

Having been diagnosed with dyslexia and doubled-vision, I have always had a tough time reading. Yet even with two strikes against me, I discovered the real problem was my inability to define a sizable portion of the words within my own vocabulary. Using the Kangaroo Method to weed out these verbal blind spots I instantly began to read with more fluency, comprehension, and retention. Today, although I still read somewhat slowly, I find myself much more able to maintain focus and interest without becoming disengaged or sleepy. I have become so much more able that I feel it is my responsibility and even my duty and mission to share what I know with others.

Unlocking Your Intelligence

Just last century scientists thought intelligence was fixed—that our I.Q. did not change. Today, neurologists agree this is simply not true. Instead of boundaries holding us back there are only frontiers in which to expand.

Verbal intelligence most certainly can be raised. In adults, however, it first needs to be unlocked. As I soon hope to convince you, it is the accumulation of verbal blind spots holding you back from your rightful intelligence. I have found clear words and personal observations are to a reader as opportune winds and calm seas are to a sailor; both allow oceans to be crossed and new lands discovered. From this point of view came a stunning realization: we may be the geniuses we innately know ourselves to be.

It is the scrutiny of commonly used words that I propose to be the golden key to unlocking verbal intelligence. There is a great difference between the present you and the child of long ago. Relying on vague or child-like understandings of vocabulary words holds verbal intelligence in check. You have grown, but has your understanding of the words you once learned in school also grown?

Sometimes it is the "small stuff" that makes the greatest of difference between average and brilliant. The average American red wine enthusiast can tell the difference between a merlot and pinot noir, whereas a wine connoisseur, from the subtlest differences in flavor and texture, can distinguish the region where a wine was produced, the year, and even perhaps the specific winery or château. In comparison, a twelve-year-old boy can tell you he has swollen glands and needs to stay home from school, whereas an astute and verbally intelligent parent knows her child has swollen lymph nodes and would be capable of defining the words "lymph" and "node."

Our problem stems from the use of too many inadequately known words. While technologies continue to advance at an ever-increasing rate, the majority of Americans still find themselves surprisingly unable to explain the term, "technology," in simple words. They have grown in experience but are not yet able to pair their competencies with an equivalent level of word power. It is one thing when a teenager cannot define the terms "algebra" and "art". It is quite another thing when the teen's parent or teacher cannot.

CHAPTER TWO

Developing Learning Strength and Know-How

HAVE you ever watched an artist in action? While attending an arts festival a few years ago, I carefully observed an artist rendering a charcoal sketch of a young girl. Skillfully, he drew an oval, outlining the head, then the neck and flowing hairline. Next, with particular attention to the general features of her face, he outlined the shape of the girl's eyes, nose, lips, and chin. Finally, he added lighter lines and shadows, bringing the portrait of the lovely young girl to completion. Then he ripped the page from his sketchbook and presented it to the girl and her parents. They were thrilled, and I was inspired. Within minutes, he had revealed the best way to present a subject to the human mind: sequentially, outlining the topic to gain an overview, adding the key features, detailing the specifics within the framework, and presenting the final summary.

This insight, about the importance of beginning any

endeavor by focusing on the big picture, is understood by education experts—and, if you think about it, many of us instinctively, as well. For example, if a friend unexpectedly pulled up in front of your house and said, "Get in," you would naturally want to know where she was planning on taking you and how long it would take. Pilots, before ever taking off, begin with a flight plan and preflight check. And authors typically start by outlining their topics.

The fact is: Learning works best by initially grasping the outline or overview of a topic. Education experts refer to this as, "getting the big picture" or "overviewing a subject." Outlining helps the mind form a framework to which the parts and pieces of the subject may then be attached.

But because there are different types of learners, some people tend to do this naturally—while the rest of us benefit from teaching ourselves how to do it.

What Type Of Learner Are You?

There are generally thought to be two kinds of learners. Some experts refer to these types as "global learners" and "sequential learners." Global learners are best at gaining the big picture, whereas sequential learners excel in following along in a logical, step-by-step manner in order to understand.

Perhaps the more common description, however, is "right-brained" and "left-brained." Right-brained people, like global learners, tend to be creative—while left-brained people, like sequential learners, tend to be more logical.

Some researchers even compare the different kinds of learners with the characteristics of the feminine and masculine energies, as well as the traditional Chinese philosophy of complementary forces, Yin and Yang.

Whether you think of yourself as a global learner or sequential learner, right-brained or left-brained, what matters is this: Every one of us tends to have a natural strength in one or the other way of perceiving the world. Neither one, in itself, is better than the other. Rather, each one is simply more appropriate for certain tasks. And most important, you can boost your intelligence and ability to be the person you want to be by identifying which method of learning is your strongest one — and then developing the other. Combating deficiencies is common practice, after all, for nutritionists, personal trainers, and coaches. Why would it be any different in education? It isn't — although not everyone recognizes that.

The act of reading is most definitely sequential: one word followed by another word in a logical manner. Interestingly enough, the term "logic" not only refers to a left-brained trait but also the word was coined from the root word, "logos," which literally means "word." Originally, the idea of being logical meant to think, speak, and write in words arranged in a sequential order that made sense. This left-brain trait forces the creative person to conform to conventional learning. Creative people will find the key to traditional education along with the skill of reading is the dedicated strengthening of their brain's word-based hemisphere.

When I was a child in public school, teachers had

twelve years to teach me three basic skills: to read, to count, and to properly express my ideas in words. In retrospect, those twelve years were not a resounding success! The first book I read from cover to cover was at age 20, my writing was awful, and I was unable to balance a checking account. As someone who considers himself right-brained, whatever success I've had in reading since then has been self-taught. Rather than relying on whatever ideas I could glean from scanning the covers of a book or listening to others, I found by shoving my attention down into the line-after-line chore of reading, I more than quadrupled my understanding. However, I also found myself constantly tuning out, losing interest, and falling asleep if the material was anything more advanced than the *National Enquirer*. I forced myself to read but found it to be an extremely uncomfortable experience—until I discovered the Kangaroo Method, and the importance of beginning with an overview in mind.

Learning From the Giants

To paint the Sistine Chapel's ceiling, Michelangelo must have both envisioned it (right-brained) and mastered the skill to paint it, stroke after stroke (left-brained). Similarly, Galileo conceived a global concept of Earth circling around the sun (right-brained) as he avidly studied mathematics through which he proved his theory (left-brained). Perhaps a person's genius manifests when both hemispheres become developed.

Grasping The Big Picture: In Five Easy Steps

You will not, of course, want or need to overview every book before you read it. There are some books that we are meant to lose ourselves in. Novels and inspirational books, for example, are best read cover-to-cover, allowing the author to take charge of the journey. But if you are reading a book to develop specific need-to-know information for school or work; to learn about the world of science, art, or any other body of knowledge; or simply to gain some practical knowledge, I have found that these five overviewing steps will help you learn the material much faster and more effectively.

Step One: Think Like Indiana Jones

If Indiana Jones were encountering an ancient scroll containing exotic symbols, pictographs, or signs, he would not immediately dive into a careful examination of one symbol or sign after another. Rather, he would maintain a healthy distance and try to take it all in — the way you take in a friend's whole face in a flash, not sequentially looking from left to right and top to bottom. In other words, he would rely on his brain's right hemisphere, the place that allows us to gain a flash of instant understanding. This is similar to the feeling you have when you gaze at a beautiful oil painting, listen to your favorite song, or get the punch line of a joke.

In reading, I think of this as cultivating the feeling of "book-time." Book-time is a feeling of being in the same moment as the author. For instance, imagine I am communicating this sentence to you—right now—as you are reading. Although logically, it may be challenging to envision both of us being here in the same moment, there is a part of you that is able to feel our connection in this moment. It is what spiritual masters refer to as the "Now." By taking a few seconds to *feel* our connection in book-time, your right hemisphere will rev up and be ready to fire all-at-once understandings.

Of course, to truly understand, you will need both parts of the brain: the creative and the rational or sequential. You need the sequential part of your brain to decode the words on a page and the global part to grasp all-at-once concepts. The importance is having *both* engines running smoothly at the start of a learning experience. By cultivating what may be the weaker of your two sides of the brain, you can enable both hemispheres to work effectively in concert.

Step Two: Establish a Goal

Open your journal or notebook and write down the date, the book's title and author, and where you are now. Then write down your reason for reading. This establishes purpose and thereby focuses your attention.

For example, if the book is a textbook assigned by a professor, you can write: "My goal is to pass all assignments and tests on this material." If the book is a self-study project on the fundamentals of negotiation, you can write: "My goal is to isolate and list specific negotiation fundamentals." If the book is work-related, you can write down what you'll be doing with the information, such as, "My goal is to integrate this new computer program into our billing system."

It is the purpose that dictates how much of the book to read and determines the depth of your study. It will help you gauge how much attention to pay to details, what to commit to memory, and what you will need to do with the information you are learning.

To put it another way, scuba divers learn to plan their dive and dive their plan. I am suggesting planning your reading dive before diving your plan. By making your purpose clear at the outset, your brain will become focused on what it is after and motivated to go after it. Plan your dive, dive your plan.

Step Three: Take 15 Minutes to Overview

To overview a chapter, give yourself a few minutes to skim the first paragraph and write down any keywords you find, paying close attention to how each keyword is pronounced and spelled. (You can listen to the pronunciations of words at dictionary.com)

Then skim the first two sentences of each of the remaining paragraphs. You can do this somewhat haphazardly as your only goal is to gain a fast—not a comprehensive—understanding of the chapter's content.

Finally, skim the last paragraph in its entirety. And if a relevant question arises for you, jot it down.

Skimming is a quick, light reading style that passes over specific details of a subject. Like a plane flying above the clouds during bad weather, fly over anything that starts tugging at your attention. If there is an obvious unknown word that seems important, simply write it in your journal, once more paying attention to its pronunciation and spelling.

Adopt a mildly skeptical attitude. Skeptical people grasp ideas well but rarely buy into beliefs. While talking with them, you may notice it feels as if they are energetically preventing themselves from being sold on an idea. This tough attitude works perfectly while skimming though a chapter because it keeps you from being pulled deeper into the subject.

Use a finger or a pen tip while gliding across the sentences. Like a cat following a string, this action pulls your eyes along. You are there strictly to get what you can get on this first pass, not to become bogged down by details.

Informational authors usually explain the general content of a chapter in the first paragraph and may revisit it during the last paragraph. The first and last paragraphs can give you the chapter overview in the *author's words*. The secret to building an effective overview is to grasp this "big idea" in the author's words and then reconstruct it in your own words. It's just like listening to someone say something and then saying it back in your own words. Or likewise, watching someone *do* something and then doing it yourself.

You will have a fair sense of the big idea after reading the first and last paragraphs. However, there is an extra important advantage to additionally skimming the first couple of sentences throughout the chapter prior to writing down your understanding of the big idea. A paragraph, after all, represents one idea. And authors neatly organize their ideas in paragraph form, one followed by the next.

Informational authors usually begin each paragraph with a sentence or two intended to convey the gist of that paragraph's idea. By skimming the first two sentences, you will effectively touch on each of the chapter's ideas and thus become familiar with the chapter. Even more importantly, you'll establish the physical location for all the individual ideas. This is the key to becoming able to rapidly hunt down specific information relating to your purpose.

Step Four: Research Keywords

After skimming the first and last paragraph in their entirety, and the first couple of sentences of every paragraph in between, it's time to research the keywords you wrote down in your journal. Look them up and identify the origin of these words.

Tip: I use two online sources—

Dictionary.com and etymonline.com; and two print sources—*American Heritage Dictionary* and *Encarta College Dictionary*.

Keywords (and key phrases) are the most important words within any subject because these are the terms that represent the actual parts and pieces of the subject. Researching their origins allow you to make the keywords easier to grasp.

Take, for example, the term "igneous" [ig-nee-us]. Igneous is one of the three categories of rock and, as a result, one of the principal parts that make up the subject called, "petrology," [pi-**trol**-*uh*-jee], which is the scientific study of rocks (from petro- meaning, "rock or stone," and –ology meaning, "the study of.") The origin of "igneous" means "fire." Lava from a volcano is on fire. As it cools down and hardens, it forms igneous rock.

By examining their origins, keywords simplify, allowing the right brain to get it, fast! An analogy for this simplifying technique is to observe what happens to a campfire when you toss in a huge chunk of wood. It dampens the flame. Split the chunk up into smaller pieces and the campfire is more able to handle the fuel without losing momentum. Likewise, by breaking down any complex term into its root and prefix or grasping the original meaning of a word, tends to ignite understanding.

By the way, "ignite" and "igneous" are two words coined from the same Latin root. "Petroleum" comes from "petro-" and "oleum" ("oil"), and literally means, "rock oil." By researching the humble beginnings (or history) of important terms, we become better able to connect big words to real life.

With today's advances in technology, innovators are continually coining new words and phrases. By taking an extra moment to go behind the scenes in order to discover how or why a particular word or phrase was chosen to represent an important concept actually simplifies the term by activating relevant background knowledge. You get the feeling, "Oh, that makes sense!"

Did You Know?

"Bluetooth" comes from the name of a tenth-century king who is remembered for uniting a group of warring Scandinavian tribes. Today, Bluetooth provides a short-range radio system serving to unite competing Internet and mobile devices.

By examining the origin of a word or gaining insight into why a term was so chosen or coined allows important words and phrases to become part of your high-definition vocabulary and not just some word you learned by rote.

Step Five:
Write an Overview in Your Own Words

The last step is to write a short statement about what a chapter covers in words that make sense to you.

Here, for example, is something I wrote in my journal about one of my favorite subjects, rocks:

"Rocks are pieces of Earth's hard crust. They are formed three ways:

1. Igneous (fire) is molten (melted) rock that cools (ex: granite).
2. Sedimentary (to settle, sit) are small pieces of dead plants, animals, and minerals that settle on

the bottom of the ocean and compress together into layers (ex: shale, sandstone).

3. Metamorphic (between forms) is any type of existing rock that sits around for thousands of years deep inside the lower crust of Earth and is subjected to both intense heat and pressure. These rocks slowly morph (become transformed) into a very solid rock form (e.g., limestone turns into marble). Thus, rocks are made from heat and/or pressure. They all eventually break apart and reform into the same or different types. This is called "the rock cycle."

Crunching down new ideas into concise sentences is tough work. I'm sure our festival artist spent time and effort developing his ability to outline a charcoal portrait. Likewise, it takes time and effort to become skilled at reshaping an author's overview into your favorite words. But I can assure you it is very much worth the effort, enabling you to eventually excel at expressing your ideas in high definition.

I'll never forget the day my parents, disappointed by my grades, made me promise to work harder in school. I sincerely promised to do my best. But the sad fact of the matter was, I had no real idea how to work harder. I just sat at my desk staring harder at the pages of a textbook. After all, I had never received any formal classroom instruction on how to study. Had I known these steps then, I could have learned more, rather than simply strain my eyes.

CHAPTER THREE

The Kangaroo Method

WORDS come easily to some people. They take to them like other people take to music or sports. But for me, reading and listening to teachers used to be the hardest way to learn. Perhaps you know the feeling, especially if you have taken a class at the college level. Professors often use words many of us have a fair sense of, yet are unable to accurately define. Thus, we acknowledge their ideas during lectures and then struggle with their questions during exams. This dichotomy has led some students to think they were created with an intellectual deficit and are incapable of learning at the college level. But I believe — I know from experience — they are mistaken.

The Kangaroo Method is designed to help you spot vocabulary terms you feel you know but are at loss to define. These words act as blind spots and hold you back from realizing your full potential. They are words you have a surface understanding about: You feel confident with them, are able to use them properly in sentences, and rightfully assume you know them. However, you don't know them well enough to adequately define them in your own simple words. They were learned by rote when you were just a child and are not a part of your high-definition adult vocabulary.

I believe that these inadequately known words, or verbal blind spots, create the illusion of limited intelligence by preventing adults from understanding material at the college level. They keep you from realizing your rightful intelligence—your own natural genius—in the here and now. But they need not.

After all, what you know is equal in value to what you don't know. What you know you can explain and show. What you don't know creates curiosity. Curiosity generates interest, and interest is the glue that holds your attention on the page.

From this day forward, you need only to clarify questionable definitions. By doing so, you will begin to achieve the reading fluency, comprehension, focus, and retention you seek. Just as high musical intelligence allows musicians to perform a note with its proper pitch and tone, high verbal intelligence allows a reader to define a word with its proper contextual definition. Words and word pieces are the building blocks of verbal intelligence.

Your success takes the willingness to observe when you tune out, and to identify and look up the words you have yet to fully understand. There is no need to make a big deal of this or to change your present direction. Just do your best to allow your brain to do its job. By becoming a watcher of words, you will stay more alert and in control of your learning process.

The Kangaroo Method requires you to become more aware of the mental changeover from phrases, sentences, and paragraphs into thoughts and ideas. In short, it calls on you to first, notice when you tune out; second, try to explain the meaning of what you are reading in your own words; and, third, look up what you don't know, and then check for understanding again. What follows will explain how.

Step One: Notice When You Tune Out

Reading is a little bit like driving a car. As you drive down the street, one part of your brain is handling the steering wheel, gas pedal and brake, while the other part is paying attention to what's happening around you—or, perhaps to what's for dinner, how to pay the bills, or how many days it will be until Friday.

If your mind happens to pass by an inadequately known word, it causes a disruption, just like a bump in the road. Your attention cuts out for a fraction of a second. When your attention re-engages it is likely to shift tracks for a moment. This is tune out. Your eyes will still be making their way down the page but your mind is somewhere else.

It is natural, of course, for our minds to wander. In the book, *Universe in a Nutshell,* physicist Stephen Hawking wrote that the human brain has millions of processors working at the same time. As a result, all it takes is one important, inadequately known word or phrase to momentarily pop your attention off the page. The mind shifts over to thinking about some other present time interest or concern. Moreover, this happens so fast, we are often completely unaware that it has happened.

Within a few seconds, it may dawn on you that you were reading. Then your attention shifts back, and you are off running again until the next time you go by something else you don't know. Depending on the number of poorly known words you encounter, your attention may be shifting about a lot!

Have you ever gotten to the bottom of a page and completely forgotten what you just read? Or, felt like you were fully tracking with an author and then suddenly felt less engaged? You started off excited about what you are reading but ended up getting sleepy. This happens in classrooms all the time! You might be sitting there listening to a lecture, and all of a sudden you get the feeling that you just came back from somewhere. Heck, you don't even know where you've been! You were listening one moment—and then gone. The feeling is similar to coming to while driving on an Interstate highway and realizing your attention was somewhere else for the last few miles.

Why We Tune Out

We tune out for many reasons. First, words stimulate emotions, and emotions can get in the way of intellectual understanding. If you happened to be studying sociology and ran across the word, "evil," it might stir up a bad feeling—and the emotional inflammation caused by the mere mention of this word could overtake your intellect.

Second, your brain can be temporarily unfit or bogged down with a personal problem. In this instance, quite frankly, you aren't even in the ballpark of quality learning. Provided you don't have other things going on—such as being sleep deprived, hungry, intoxicated or drugged, dehydrated, out of shape, rushed and under pressure, or have an all consuming problem robbing your attention— you should be able to notice an instance of tuning out as you pass by a word or phrase you need to know better.

Third, we have awesome imaginations. The brain is very quick to fire up an idea, even when a key word is unknown. It does so by its ability to analyze the word within the context and then to piece together its best guess. However, what we conjecture may not always match the meaning the author intends.

And finally, as you read a word you need to know better, your attention may simply snag on the term and disrupt your comprehension. As you continue to read, the snagged term will quickly disappear from your thoughts; and as it disappears, it will take with it some of your attention or mental energy. This is what you need to learn to notice.

Consciousness is more like a light bulb hooked up to a dimmer switch than an on-and-off switch. Unknown words dim you down, and your mind becomes unable to stay focused. Soon, you will find your mind wandering as your eyes faithfully work their way down the page.

Stages of Tune Out

The first stage is the initial disconnection. You can usually sense your mind snagging on an unknown word provided you are generally alert and well rested. If you are using an electronic reader, click on the word, grab the meaning and move on in the text.

The second is semi-unconsciousness. I can't tell you the number of times I've drifted down a page or even through an entire section or half-chapter while thinking about something else altogether. Once I catch myself, I stop and try to find my point of departure. Depending on how long I was "out," it may take a few moments to locate the paragraph and the word that knocked me out. When I find it, I become energized and refocused again.

The Kinds of Words We Tune Out To

The types of words your mind tunes out to may surprise you. You would think the words that cause tune out are the big, huge technical words. And, sure, they will pop your attention off the page if you go flying by them. But you know you don't know these words and are probably hoping the author will offer an explanation a bit further down the page. The worst ones are the words you assume you know but don't!

On the other hand, your mind won't tune out to every poorly known word. In the phrase, "it's such a nice day," few people can define the word "such." But who cares? It is the *important* words within key phrases that cause us to tune out.

If an important word is left undefined, the phrase containing the word will fail to fire properly resulting in the entire sentence becoming hard to understand. You will think you don't understand the entire sentence or idea, when in fact the cause was just one or two key terms you didn't know well enough. It's like thinking something is very wrong with your car when the problem boils down to a couple of bad plugs!

The Kangaroo Standard

The Kangaroo Method is the deliberate separation between known and unknown vocabulary terms by use of a specific standard. The standard, or way in which this division is made, is by a simple rule-of-thumb: If you can explain a word within its context, you know the word. But if you can't say in relatively simple terms what a word means, you don't know the word well enough.

As Albert Einstein said, "If you can't explain it simply, you don't understand it well enough." Physicist and Nobel Prize winner Werner Heisenberg also emphasized the importance of simple descriptions, saying: "Even for the physicist, the description in plain language will be a criterion of the degree of understanding that has been reached." The Kangaroo Method uses Einstein's "explain it simply" standard for word definitions, too! And, why not? This standard separates the known from the inadequately known.

As you first start using the Kangaroo Method, the words you locate and define are the more obvious unknown words. As your awareness increases, however, more and more inadequately known common words will start to surface. When you start to notice instances of tuning out, see if you can catch what caused your mind to jump tracks. It could be as simple as you didn't hear a word; there was a sudden noise that startled you; or something someone said reminded you of a related experience. But you can get good at picking up these moments. And by catching and fixing these little glitches, I think you'll be amazed at the difference it will make in your ability to learn with much more alertness and comprehension.

What's In a Name?

The Kangaroo Method takes its name from a common myth about the origin of the word "kangaroo." According to legend, Captain James Cook and naturalist Sir Joseph Banks were exploring a remote region in Australia when they happened across an unusual animal with powerful hind legs, underdeveloped forelegs, and a long heavy tail that carried its young in an abdominal pouch.

Wanting to find out what the locals called this creature, they asked an aboriginal man who replied "gangurru." Mistakenly, they took the term to be the name of the creature and recorded it as kangooroo or kanguru. But, in fact, it meant: "I don't understand you."

The Kangaroo Method is the "I don't understand you" method. Once practiced, this tool can allow you to gain a much deeper and more practical understanding of the world around you.

Case-in-Point: What the Heck is a Vowel?

As young children, we all learned our vowels: a, e, i, o, and u. By vocalizing the vowels and writing them down we have shown that we know them. However, are you easily able to explain what a vowel is? When I ask people to define "vowel," many will say:

> "A vowel is a letter that is not a consonant." But that is what a vowel is *not*. So what is a vowel? Many people then answer: "A vowel connects consonants."
> But that is what a vowel *does*. So, again, what *is* a vowel?

To their surprise, most people come up blank. Reluctantly, they surrender the term to the unknown. The act of surrendering is like placing the transmission of your car in neutral. Inside your mind, surrendering a word as not known is similar to shifting your car's transmission from "drive" through neutral to "reverse." When one surrenders a word to the unknown, the mind passes through a moment of silence as it shifts gears from a state of assured belief to a state of focused curiosity. It is the shift from, "I know this!" to "What the heck is a vowel?" that creates an instantaneous desire to learn.

The sudden recognition of not knowing the definition of an "everybody knows" word comes as a surprise for most people. This is their first experience of uncovering a verbal blind spot. The experience can be somewhat destabilizing for the ego. But then, once the shift has taken place, curiosity demands a basic definition for the word. Prior to receiving the dictionary definition, many students get an absent look on their faces like they are missing a personal object such as their car keys or cell phone and are trying to remember where they put it. Others look as though they are working to piece together a definition. Either way, they become curious about what the dictionary has to say. Curiosity is the feeling of recognizing or beholding an unknown and is the fuel of self-motivated learning.

In fact, a vowel is a speech sound where the voiced breath is not stopped with the tongue, teeth, or lips. In other words, vowels are vocal sounds that go through the mouth without stopping the airflow, whereas consonants are the vocal sounds that are partially or wholly stopped using the tongue, teeth, or lips.

When my students learn this, most start to laugh and freely admit they had never learned this definition. Then they enthusiastically begin uttering the various vowel sounds and become curious about the letter "y." I offer the words "monkey" and "yellow" to demonstrate the vowel and consonant sounds. I wish you could see them: a room full of professional adults laughing and asking questions about an elementary school word that somehow slipped by without ever being fully understood. In that moment, it is as if their childlike curiosity has become refreshed—and their verbal intelligence unlocked.

Let's face it: People are smart. For most of us, it takes only the discovery of one verbal blind spot to understand the difference between knowing something on a surface level and knowing it in "high definition." From then on, they become watchers of words. If they can't say what a word means, they quickly look it up before moving on in the text. They have consciously and willingly slowed down to take back control of their learning process. An awareness of having been unaware is all it takes.

Why It Matters

Inevitably, someone also asks why it matters whether they know the definition of a word they are able to identify. They suggest that their ability to list or show vowels, for example, is good enough. And perhaps, in the case of one word, it is. But it is the total accumulation of verbal blind spots that form the hidden barrier to learning and impairs your ability to learn at the traditional college level. One word is like the tip of an iceberg. It is the unknown mass that sends a ship and its crew into the abyss—or, if revealed, on a grand adventure.

Step Two: See If You Can Explain It In Your Own Words

A few years ago, I was reading a science article about how the various types of rocks are created in nature. Shortly after starting to read, I noticed my attention started to wander. Realizing I had tuned out, I looked back over the previous two paragraphs hoping to find a word that caused the initial disconnection. One sentence stood out:

"With few exceptions, such as coal, rocks consist of one or more minerals."

The sentence made sense, although I was feeling slightly less engaged and somewhat glib. I noticed on my desk there was a stone, a small rounded rock I had found earlier that year while wandering along a beach in Sandwich, Massachusetts. Holding the stone in my hand, I looked closely while considering it to be made of minerals. Suddenly it dawned on me, I was at a complete loss to explain the word mineral. All I could immediately think of was "vitamins and minerals."

Refusing to accept that I didn't know this word, my brain started sifting through memories in an attempt to cobble together a definition. I remembered the pure white sands of Cozumel, Mexico. I recalled zooming in on one grain of sand and pondering the countless atoms and molecules that came together to form this tiny piece of matter. Next, an image appeared of an abandoned gold mine in the mountains northwest of Denver where, at age 25, I spent an hour feverishly breaking apart rocks containing rose quartz and sprinklings of gold. The words "mining" and "ore" came to mind.

As I considered these thoughts, I was still unable to put my finger on the gist of the term, mineral. I knew that ore consisted of minerals containing intermittent metals, such as gold or silver and were, of course, made up of atoms and molecules. I attempted to put an explanation together by saying a mineral is "a hardened physical substance made up of atoms and molecules." But this definition was complex, far too general, and much too abstract.

Once more it hit me: I had no idea how to express the word mineral in simple terms. Stuff dug out of a mine? Sure, but what stuff? My mind was drawing a blank.

I finally surrendered the word. The moment of silence and shift in thinking caused me to suddenly feel more awake. I remembered my little box of minerals I had as a child. Each mineral was glued to a white card just above its name. The card was perfectly fitted into the bottom of a shallow, dark green display box. From deep within me, a child's voice whispered the question: "What is a mineral?"

Here was a basic science term I had first come across in elementary school and was now appearing almost foreign! It took only a few seconds to grasp its meaning after I looked it up. Minerals are "all the little hard things that have never been alive."

"That's right," my inner child exclaimed, "Plants, animals, and minerals!" I reviewed the passage again, and it immediately made sense. My prior feelings of boredom and disconnection vanished as a rush of energy filled my head. Curious, I checked out the definition of coal and found it to be exactly as I had thought: "a rock made from highly compressed plant matter." I again picked up my little rock and said to myself, "Compressed minerals! How about that?"

The word "mineral" had been a verbal blind spot that existed within me for years. It was a word I was taught as a child but never fully captured. Finding and correcting this single verbal blind spot reawakened my interest in Earth Science. A few months later, I took an Earth Science class online and remember being in awe of how our planet renews itself from the viewpoint of geological time.

No one can tell you which words are verbal blind spots for you. You will have to discover them for yourself. But by using the Kangaroo Method, which uses the phenomenon of tuning out to locate vocabulary terms you need to better know, you can achieve and maintain high definition learning on whatever subject interests you.

Step Three: Look It Up— And Check Again For Meaning

Imagine you are studying the colonial history of the United States and come across the following sentence: "With the passing of the calumet, tensions eased among the men of the two nations."

What do you think "calumet" means in this context?

I once had a dairy farmer in one of my classes who thought he heard: "the cow you met." Another student thought "calumet" was a kidney stone that had passed. Some people have thought it referred to someone who passed away. And most people—perhaps you, too—have thought it refers to a treaty or agreement.

The word calumet, in fact, means "peace pipe."

Now read the sentence again: "With the passing of the calumet, tensions eased among the men of the two nations."

Did you notice your idea of the sentence change? This is how you can clarify the thought of an author. When in doubt, check the definition of the questionable words to get the best comprehension you can, and then reread the sentence.

A Living Language

Oliver Wendell Holmes once said: "A word is not a crystal, transparent and unchanged, it is the skin of a living thought and may vary greatly in color and content according to the circumstances and the time in which it is used."

In other words, the meanings of words stretch to reflect every new generation's thoughts and serve each industry's needs. Pronunciations of technical words and phrases continue to be crunched down into fewer syllables while packing their same complexity of meaning. Buzzwords rise in fashion and, from overuse, fizzle like the tailings of aerial fireworks. Words and word pieces can be weaved together to create new meanings just as primary colors are blended to create contemporary shades.

And yet, akin to any art form, language consists of fundamentals. As a scholar, Mr. Holmes was well grounded in English, Latin, French, Spanish, and Italian. His firmly established knowledge of these Romantic languages coupled with his vast personal experience provided him the capacity to capture and delight in even the subtlest nuances of the English language. Likewise, the Kangaroo Method serves to help you get a leg up on high definition vocabulary, which in turn generates high definition reading and learning.

By becoming aware of what you don't fully understand, you can stop for a moment and check out inadequately known words. By doing so, your mind will be able to fire up ideas with much greater clarity. This is especially easy if you are using an e-book reader where you can get an instant definition by touching the term. You can use this tool, or the old-fashioned dictionary, to look up what you don't know and then check for meaning.

As Henry David Thoreau wrote: "To know that we know what we know, and that we do not know what we do not know, that is true knowledge." That is the Kangaroo Method's gold standard.

CHAPTER FOUR

To Weave Together

A T just sixteen, I sat behind the wheel of my mother's convertible, valiantly trying to parallel park. The Department of Motor Vehicles examiner sat in the seat next to me, his head down, quietly scribbling notes—until I backed into the curb. Then he quickly looked up and failed me right then and there. My father and older brother found something about my failure funny. I found it humiliating. But I was also determined to get my drivers license and asked my father, who had been a Navy pilot, for help.

After spending a few minutes thinking about it, he advised: "You have to divide parallel parking into less complicated steps. Each step will have a beginning position, its maneuver, and a finishing position. The most important thing is to make sure the finishing position is exact, because that finishing position will become the next maneuver's starting position. Your success depends upon getting each action to dovetail into the next." In short, he added, "The entire procedure just boils down to a group of individually practiced actions that are woven together."

More specifically, he said, parallel parking consists of five steps: (1) positioning your car beside the car you want to park behind; (2) reversing straight back and then turning the wheel toward the curb to achieve the proper angle; (3) reversing while straightening the wheel; (4) turning the wheel away from the curb as you reverse into a position parallel to the curb; and (5) pulling forward to the proper parked position.

He instructed me to practice each step *before* thinking about doing the whole maneuver. He took the wheel and demonstrated. Then he told me to do the same. I practiced the five short steps, one at a time, until I could do each effortlessly. Then I practiced the entire maneuver about a dozen times until I felt confident I could pass the test.

In the process, he pointed out the specific problem that made me fail the test: I was not consistently attaining the proper angle before backing into the parking space. He made me stop and walk around the car to observe the "wrong angle." Then, when I achieved the correct angle, he told me to observe the "proper angle." With a few more repetitions, I realized I had been blindly guessing at the proper angle. But once I knew it, the entire procedure became a breeze.

Thanks to this experience, I not only learned how to parallel park and passed my retest three weeks later but I learned the ingredients of building a skill that day. Even the most complex procedures my Dad taught me, can be divided into a series of short, simple movements, each of which consists of a starting position; planned and regulated movements in the middle; and an ending position.

What Is a Skill?

Simply put, a skill is an ability to do something well. Skills are what others admire in us, what earn us a living, and what will engrave our mark upon this world. It is, therefore, important to understand how these valuable habits are attained and mastered—and the full extent to which we are in charge. I believe that how good we get with the hand we were dealt is entirely up to us. How good we become at dealing with other people, handling our financial affairs, performing our job, and even reading and learning are completely under our own control.

Consider, then, the word "skill" in high definition: A skill is a unified collection of individually practiced actions that are in some way valuable.

Each action is repeated until it becomes as automatic as a reflex or habit. And within each skill, there are two types of actions: the simple and complex.

1. *Simple actions* can be quickly mastered by repeating them until they are hardwired into the brain and nervous system. For example, placing the bow of a violin on a string and drawing it across until a consistent musical note is achieved can be thought of as one simple action (albeit, one that takes practice!)
2. *Complex actions* may appear formidable but

only until we look closely at what constitutes a complex action. The root of the word "complex" is "to weave together" or "something that has been woven together." Complex actions, then, are two or more simpler actions woven together into an integrated whole, such as the playing of a musical scale. They may take a dozen or more repetitions to become embedded into the brain and nervous system, and even more to create stable connections of neural pathways. But eventually, even highly complex actions can be performed instantly as a result of repetition.

Skills are learned from top to bottom, and from bottom to top. In other words, by observing my father parallel park, I quickly grasped an overview of the procedure containing its steps: This was learning from the top to bottom. Then, I practiced each of the sequential steps and worked through the procedure as a whole—building my skills from the bottom up.

In fact, as it turns out, skill building is the same as overviewing a chapter of information and then working to grasp the details. We observe and then integrate—or weave the pieces together into a whole.

Skill Mastery

When asked which artists and scholars have influenced them, many successful people sincerely acknowledge their gratitude to those special people they once studied as part of their creative growth. We instinctively learn by mimicking those we admire. The ability to mimic is, in fact, part and parcel to success. In fact, the roots of "success" and "succession" are the same word. We watch and listen as the sequential steps are carried out in what appears to be one, interconnected pattern.

As a professional, how skilled and knowledgeable you become in your chosen field is up to you. It does not depend on anything or anyone else. Take a minute to deeply consider this point. For example, look at things within a twenty-foot radius of you right now that were made by human beings. The hands of skilled men and women have created the chair or couch you may be seating on, the book you are reading, the artwork you may be observing, and the clothes you are wearing. How competent you or I become, given physical limitations and available resources, is one of the few facts of life that are completely within our control.

Skill building, then, consists of doing. Once we mimic the actions of a step, we perceive the step as an all-at-once experience. We may think to ourselves, "I got it!" At this point, we need to repeat the actions until the step is permanently embedded into the brain and nervous system as an automatic reflex. Educators refer to this level as "unconscious competence."

Pushing Through Push Back

Anything we push against pushes back. That is why, as we attempt to practice a new series of actions, the brain and nervous system will resist the change. Yet neurologists tell us the brain does change. They use the term, "neuro-plasticity" [neuro plas **tis** ity] to suggest that the brain is moldable like plastic. Compared to the speed of thought, however, physical changes in the brain occur slowly. So you must treat the programming of your brain as you would the teaching of a young child. You need to be both patient and persistent.

By attentively and consistently repeating a short grouping of actions, the programming starts to take place. In the beginning, you may start to feel mildly or moderately irritable—just as children do when you require them to practice the same action, again and again. But as the nervous system becomes accustomed to the repetitions and accepts the indoctrination, you can rest assured that your irritability will subside.

Still, to permanently ingrain a skill, the repetitions must continue through an even tougher level of mastery. Of course, you may become bored and, as a result, easily distracted. Transient thoughts and ideas will attempt to draw our attention and we may find ourselves suddenly "remembering" to make a phone call or to take care of some other business. Determination and persistence, perhaps even some external coaching, are needed to push past this stage of mastery. Just remember: This is the make-or-break phase between mediocrity and competence.

For this reason, it is wise to select a degree program or career path that connects us to a sense of inner energy or enthusiasm (from the root, "Theo," meaning, "God," and prefix, "en" meaning, "within") because this enthusiasm will empower us to overcome whatever obstacles we may encounter as we progress along our pathway—as long as we remain honest with ourselves.

What You Fail to Master Masters You

As a twenty-one year old professional musician, I was proud of myself. I had played solo clarinet in musical ensembles in high school and college; started my own jazz quartet; and was currently playing first-chair clarinet in the United States Air Force Band. I was considered talented and was earning a living with my musical skill. There existed, however, a problem within my technical ability. On faster pieces of music, my fingers missed notes. In addition, I was unable to perform chord changes while soloing on a jazz piece. I faked my way through, never resolving the difficulty. The problem ate at me for close to two decades. My self-esteem was out the bottom but I had developed a hardened shell of false pride no one could broach. After years of frustration, I gave up music.

Perhaps you have a similar story—about something you loved and pursued but eventually gave up because you didn't feel good enough. Many of us get "just so good" at something and never quite make the transition to excellence. Why? The reason is remarkably simple: We failed to master one or more of the individually practiced actions along the way, even if our memories of these individual failures soon fade into the background.

Imagine, for example, trying to light up a performance stage in purple by combining the red and blue floodlights. No matter how many times you flip the switches, you fail to get the intended result. The solution is to identify the specific problem with the wiring—in this case, the wiring for one of the lights—and correct it. Attempting to perform any advanced technique requires its component actions to be stably woven together and fully embedded as reflex. You can't skip any of the steps and be successful.

My father helped me to locate the specific problem I was having with parallel parking. I had been blindly guessing at the proper angle while reversing into the parking spot. Once this difficulty was corrected, the entire procedure became a breeze. Unlike detecting and correcting verbal blind spots, fixing a professional skill requires a coach or teacher to help us see and resolve the specific issues.

I tell my audiences, what you have failed to master has mastered you. Each time you move beyond your true level of competency, you lose your integrity. But by understanding the simple mechanics of skill building, you can release the past and start fresh today.

CHAPTER FIVE

Hard Work and Memories

WHEN I was growing up in a middle-class family in Syracuse, New York, I knew almost nothing about my mother's family lineage. After the Second World War, Mom had fallen in love with a Navy officer. Being six years older than he, married twice previously, and already the mother of two children, they eloped to avoid repercussions, and we never had contact with her side of the family.

Yet she named me after her father, my grandfather, Dr. Donald Gardner Russell, a graduate of Yale University, who died at age 28 from influenza in France during the First World War. My great grandfather, William Samuel Russell, was also a medical doctor educated at Yale. Other Russell family members had taught at Yale for generations; and one of them, Rev. Noadiah Russell, was a founder and original trustee of Yale College. She once said she wished I had followed my family's path into medicine.

I sometimes wonder about the differences between their lives and mine. Mom's family members were people of academic accomplishment, wealth, and privilege. Was school easy for them, or were they expected to work harder than other people? How would my life have turned out if my grandfather hadn't died so young? Would I have gone to Yale instead of a state college? Was my less impressive academic achievement due to lower family expectations, my failure to work hard, or was it because I was never taught how to study?

It's funny to think back to the child we once were. We change, but many habits take root early on in life and become woven into our character. Events in elementary school can set a precedent for good or bad academic and professional habits. In first grade, for example, I came home for lunch every day. Mom would have a bowl of Campbell's soup, a sandwich, and a glass of milk set out on the table.

One day, I came home upset. The day before, my teacher, Mrs. Horton, had given us math problems to do at home. She offered no explanation of why we had to do the math work at home. And I wasn't happy about using my personal time to do school work. I hated homework! I also was more interested in gluing together a model Navy airplane like my Dad used to fly. So I never did it. And when I showed up at school that morning, I was sternly reprimanded and told I needed to finish the assignment at lunch. I was furious and resentful—and, in truth, my attitude toward homework never changed during high school or college. I raced through one assignment after another, just to get it done. The true value of homework never dawned on me until I heard myself explaining the purpose of homework to a room full of strangers.

Building Memory Skill

On a chilly Saturday morning in late November, I dressed warmly and headed off to give a presentation at a learning symposium being held at the Marriott Marquis in New York City. The morning presenters included a professor of neurology and an author of a book on how the brain works. They both had convincing PowerPoints about the brain, types of memory, and age-related memory loss problems. Jetlagged and tired after the flight in from Denver and a less-than-restful night in a cramped hotel room, I arrived an hour late, quietly taking a seat at the back of the room.

The morning speakers offered serious, academic information about the brain, while the afternoon tended to be more entertaining. After the short afternoon break, I found my way to the podium and began to introduce the Kangaroo Method, focusing, as had been requested, on practical solutions for remembering what you read. I briefly talked about how to stay tuned-in, break down complex terms, and use personal analogies to make memory connections between new information and real-life experience.

Shortly after, the program director walked to the front of the room and stood to the side of me against the wall: a signal, I presume, that it was time to sum up. Reflecting on the anxiety about memory loss that had been expressed through the day, I decided to use my final minutes to address memory as a skill. Many people worry about their memory, I said. But worrying about something tends to make it worse, not better. I don't mean to make light of the problem of memory loss. My father suffered from Alzheimer's, and I cared for my father the last years of his life. I know how difficult it can be. But I do believe that there is a practical solution for many common memory problems, and that begins with recognizing what types of things we naturally remember and then to build the skills that allow us to supplement this natural ability.

To remember, after all, means: "to piece together again." Any new and unusual life experiences, along with times of strong physical and emotional impact, become naturally imbedded deep in our memory. For example, you will naturally remember the first day you rode a horse, the day you got married, or went to Niagara Falls. But compare these high-impact experiences with some fact or procedure you need to remember to pass a test. Do you see the difference? That little fact doesn't have the same whole-brain impact as a moving, first-time life experience.

So what can you do to remember the kind of information that is difficult to retain? It's simple. You need to make a learning experience happen. You do so by talking about it, considering it, comparing it to similar ideas, writing it down in your journal, or diagramming it. And, if you need to remember something verbatim, you repeat it over and over until it is embedded into your brain. It takes hard work and repetition but it works—if you work it.

Try this: Take a spare room or a section of a room to create a home learning studio. Then spend an hour or two there when you are at your best (for me, it is usually either in the early morning or just after dinner) and study or examine closely the information you need to move ahead. Work first to grasp the ideas as simply as you can. Then work the ideas into memory through action. Make notes. Stand up and give an oral presentation. Record yourself, and then listen to the results. If you aren't happy with it, do it again. Then, write your own questions on 3x5 cards, post them on your bathroom mirror, and quiz yourself. Talk out loud and listen to yourself speak. Action and repetition creates powerful, whole-brain learning experiences that you will remember.

In short, I concluded my talk that day, your ability to remember is a gift. Bringing that gift to life comes from practicing memory-building skills. The words hit home with the audience, and with me, too. I realized that we all have the same opportunity to master our lives. Whether we go to a state university or an Ivy League school, it is the choice each one of us makes—to work hard or not—that makes the difference. As a child, homework would have afforded me that opportunity to embed that day's learning into memory. Unfortunately, I wasted many of those opportunities. But it is never too late to change—and every day presents a new choice.

After my talk, I met an old musician friend for dinner. He had become a music professor in New York City and was playing in the orchestra for the musical "Billy Elliott." He had done the hard work and turned his love of music into a successful career.

As I thought about the phrase, "hard work," I recognize how it can evoke unpleasant feelings. It can remind us of times we felt overwhelmed and confused by difficult assignments. That night, walking in a refreshing rain in New York City, I came to grips with those feelings and then released them—and I recommend the same to you. Work is simply purposeful activity. Hard is something solid. Whisper it to the kid in you.

Conclusion

WHEN I was a fourth-grader, I told my music teacher I wanted to play the bugle (largely because I wanted to march in parades.) He told me the school didn't have bugles but needed clarinet players and, before I knew what I was getting into, he stuffed a fishy-smelling clarinet mouthpiece between my teeth, told me to bite down and blow. The squeaky sound vibrated my upper teeth making my head buzz and tickle. He told me to take it home for a week and give it a try. I left carrying a long skinny case containing a tarnished nickel-plated clarinet, the mouthpiece, and a couple of used reeds.

One month later, I performed in my first concert. I was surprised and kind of nervous when my music teacher asked me to play a middle C, by myself, in front of the whole audience. He tuned up the band as well as he could and we began our Christmas performance with Jingle Bells. A few days following the concert, my mother, still proud of her son for being the clarinetist selected to tune the entire concert band, took me to a music store and rented a black plastic Bundy clarinet. She purchased a songbook, four brand new reeds, and talked about getting me some private lessons. I asked the store clerk if he had any bugles. He said he could order them but only had trumpets and cornets in stock. Not knowing what a cornet was, I fell silent.

As I look back to those days, it was as if I took a job I really didn't want but it was the only opening they had, so I made the best of it. I played the clarinet in college and the military and part time throughout my thirties. Then, one night after playing in a hotel bar in Ithaca, New York, I broke down my expensive ebony clarinet into its five pieces, swabbed out the spit, and packed it away for the last time. I never played again.

I spent several months after that in mid-life contemplation. I came to terms with my lack of technical skill on the clarinet, realized I wasn't happy being married, and hated my sales job even though it brought in good money. I drank too much, worked too little, and felt invisible as a back-to-school adult at the local community college. I desperately needed to redefine myself. Yet on the other hand, my sales job had taught me how to talk with and present ideas to people. My ex-wife has reappeared in my life as my closest friend. And looking back, I did get to march in parades and once backed up Tony Bennett singing our national anthem. I realized life does work. If we pay attention, life does give us what we want. I just needed to get a whole lot better at defining what I wanted from it.

The Silver Bullets of Education

During my second season on tour with the Kangaroo Method, I presented a three-hour learning strategies seminar at the University of Texas at Austin. While discussing the section on the importance of being able to define words in simple terms, a student challenged me, with a slight tone of irritation: "I am here to get learning strategies. I plan to go back to college in the fall to become a lawyer. Are you saying the only thing I need to do to succeed is to be able to define words?"

I was taken off guard. Her question seemed to collapse my proposal into nothing more than looking up some words in a dictionary—hardly novel advice. So what else did I have to help her get through law school? In those early days, I remember this question being tough to answer. It would be years before I used phrases like "verbal blind spots" and "high definition" to describe the cognitive learning process. At that time, the Kangaroo Method was in its infancy and pretty much was what this student was suggesting, plus the addition of "tuning out" to help identify unknown words.

Yet I knew there existed a far richer and more insightful level of understanding achievable from well-known words coupled with related life experience. While attempting to explain the concept, however, I sounded more like an elementary teacher saying, "Class, be sure to look up the words you don't know." But it was true! I had spent years in a dictionary cracking open the meanings of words I couldn't define. More importantly, I had learned how to recognize the difference between the words I knew by rote and those I knew at the college level. As an adult learning a new subject, I found well-defined words made the difference between clarity and stupidity. By fine-tuning word definitions and understanding origins, tests and exams were actually fun to take and conversations with professors about speculative points within their subjects became almost collaborative. And it wasn't just me who found words to be silver bullets to cognitive learning.

A longtime friend, who had used the Kangaroo Method to study money and markets, became a multimillionaire and to this day claims his success was due to looking up those words. By that time, there were hundreds of other people who told me the Kangaroo Method made them twice as smart; and yet I found myself unable to convince this pre-law student of the momentous value of becoming truly word smart. There I was on stage, at the same mediocre degree of competence, it seemed, as when I last played the clarinet a decade before.

"Well, yes," I began, "words are the principal carriers of meaning, and the ability to describe the keywords of a subject is tantamount to learning that subject. For instance, you mention you are interested in becoming a lawyer. In simple terms, how would you define the term, 'law?'"

I regretted my question the moment I asked it.

After hemming and hawing over the definition of "law" for a half-minute, she blasted back, "I don't think any of my future clients will give a shit if I can or can't define the word, law, as long as I can get them off, scot-free!" She folded her arms as if to rest her case. The room went silent.

As I had suspected, she was unable to define the word. But it was a mistake to make her look stupid in front of thirty other adults.

The ability to define words and concepts is a skill. It is a skill American education fails to develop in students. In truth, when I first discovered this missing link in public education, I was shocked. If you think about it, outside of essays and short-answer tests, academic testing primarily consists of multiple choice, true and false questions, and problem solving. Vocabulary is evaluated by multiple choice and matching tests. Students are rarely required to explain the definition of a vocabulary word, only match it to a synonym or antonym. As a result, kids are able to pass through twelve years of school without adequately developing their ability to explain concepts in their own words. Since vocabulary underlies the skill of reading, it is no wonder test scores are so poor. This is the blind spot in our education. If kids were encouraged to verbally define words rather than merely matching them, they would learn to express definite under-standings in their own words. By doing so, they would greatly increase their reading comprehension.

For the average person, the word law evokes an idea of "right and wrong behavior." For an individual with high verbal intelligence, such as Thomas Jefferson, who studied Latin and Greek and became a lawyer by reading the law, the answer might be "the rules of conduct laid down and fixed within a society." He undoubtedly would have known that the word law originated from a verb meaning, "to lay down or fix."

The Most Important Idea You Will Ever Define

Words are more than vocal sounds and clusters of alphabetic symbols used to share our thoughts and ideas. They are the very means of molding our understandings and beliefs about each other, God, and the world. The way in which moms and dads define God, the physical world, and even the neighbors next door form beliefs through which their children view life. As kids mature, they become aware of differences in how others define God, each other, and the world. In our left-brained dominant society, definitions create beliefs.

For example, if we define animals as "soulless creatures," we will believe this to be true and, as a result, view the devastation of their natural habitats and confinement and harsh treatment without troubling our conscience about it. However, by changing the definition of the word animal to its original definition—"a living being that breathes and has a soul"—we will become intolerant of such abuses.

Similarly, defining a homeless person as "a worthless drug addict or lazy jobless person" allows us to pass by without the slightest care. Those who more kindly define our homeless brothers and sisters both believe and act differently. Left-brained sequential definition generates right-brained belief, which instantaneously adjusts the focus of how we see the world. We see the world through our beliefs and focus only on the evidences to support our definitions and beliefs.

Our inner self is infinite, not definite. We cannot

see ourselves as infinite because we are observing life through the looking glass of our definitions and beliefs. To understand our infinite selves, we look into the world around us and feel a sense of joy and excitement from those things that most reflect our infinite nature. We are drawn to occupations and educational pursuits that bring us into harmony with our infinite selves. Through joy and enthusiasm, we begin to define ourselves as that which most represents who we are. At age thirty-eight, I had not yet defined myself in a way that fully reflected my inner feeling of joy. My life, although viewed by others as somewhat successful, left me wanting and sad. It took courage to change the definition of myself from clarinet player and salesman to teacher and educational program director. I had no educational background or experience when I opened an adult education school and developed the courses I now teach. It just brought me tremendous joy to do so, and I found this path remarkably easy to follow. By changing how I defined myself, I became the person I wanted to be.

Learning is the combination of defining the key points of a subject and repeating the relevant ideas and actions of the subject until knowledge and competence are achieved. Subjects are shaped and defined from the top to bottom, and their related skills are taught from the bottom to top. Simply put, learning is a matter of definition and repetition—whether it is an academic subject or the subject of one's life.

It has been said that life is a process: a series of actions directed towards a specific aim. I believe the process of life is to define ourselves as closely as we can to reflect the inner joy of who we are. "Education" itself is derived from the word "educe", which means: "to draw forth from within." We move forward by gaining insights and developing skills in the field of our choosing. Though education, we become professional in those fields that reflect this inner joy.

For many adults, financial pressures can take the joy out of living by causing them to be afraid to change the definition of themselves. However, we owe the world nothing but to become the people we most wish to be and then to give back. By becoming the people of our choosing, we somehow find the means of support. Not all ships cross calm seas. Storms can rage yet also subside, and the sun eventually reappears.

We are the chemists of our own future. We decide what knowledge to integrate within our brains and bodies to become the people we most want to be. The truth is—you can change any belief about yourself to reflect your inner joy. To change a belief, change your definition. To learn any subject, discover the definitions and master the actions. It is that simple. The actions of learning a subject are equivalent to the actions involved in creating your character and your life. It is a matter of clearly defining it and repeating it into existence. You are completely free to do so and this is the one absolute you control in life.

Learning is the pathway to becoming the person you most want to be.